W9-BVL-242

THE HOW AND WHY WONDER BOOK OF
THE AMERICAN REVOLUTION

Written by FELIX SUTTON
Illustrated by LEONARD VOSBURGH
Editorial Production: DONALD D. WOLF

Edited under the supervision of
Dr. Paul E. Blackwood, Washington, D.C.

Text and illustrations approved by
Oakes A. White, Brooklyn Children's Museum, Brooklyn, New York

PRICE/STERN/SLOAN
Publishers, Inc., Los Angeles
1985

Introduction

John Adams prophesied that the anniversary of Independence Day would be celebrated by succeeding generations of Americans with bells, guns and sports. His prophecy was correct. But today's celebrations of the fourth of July sometimes fail to stimulate an appreciation of the years of strife that led up to the Declaration of Independence, and the years of war that followed it. This *How and Why Wonder Book of the American Revolution* gives the reader a new sense of how those early years are important to our present national life.

Each year, thousands of tourists visit Valley Forge, Bunker Hill, Concord, Ticonderoga and Yorktown. They see historic markers of important battles of the Revolutionary War. Visiting these places and reading the markers give a glimpse of the courage and dedication of the men and women who sought independence for a new nation. But the impressive story of the war in all its aspects is probably best understood from books, such as this one, which narrate the sequence of the events leading to the war, and of the war itself.

We are told that the American army managed to win the war chiefly by a series of lucky breaks. But surely a part of Colonists' good fortune was the presence of courageous and intelligent men such as George Washington, Patrick Henry, Thomas Paine, Thomas Jefferson and Benjamin Franklin. The part played by these and other men in the early history of our nation is highlighted for young readers by this *How and Why Wonder Book of the American Revolution.*

Paul E. Blackwood

Copyright © 1963 by Price/Stern/Sloan Publishers, Inc.
Published by Price/Stern/Sloan Publishers, Inc.
410 North La Cienega Boulevard, Los Angeles, California 90048

Printed in the United States of America. All rights reserved. No part of this publication may be reproduced, stored in a retrieval system, or transmitted, in any form or by any means, electronic, mechanical, photocopying, recording, or otherwise, without the prior written permission of the publishers.

ISBN: 0-8431-4280-4

How and Why Wonder Books is a trademark of Price/Stern/Sloan Publishers, Inc.

Contents

Cities sprang up rapidly in the prosperous colonies. This is how Battery Park in New York City looked on a Sunday afternoon in the year 1768.

What was America like after the French and Indian War?

The Seeds of Revolution

The French and Indian War, which ended in 1763, established nearly all of what is now the United States east of the Mississippi River, as British territory. The French armies had been driven out of North America, and no longer threatened the northern and western frontiers. Now, the colonists thought, they could devote themselves to the peaceful pursuit of carving a civilization out of the wilderness.

By far the greater portion of this vast

Fine craftsmen were building many sailing ships in New England for the rapidly increasing trade with England. At right, a scene in a Massachusetts harbor.

About 1750 only a few of the colonists like Benjamin Franklin (above) and Samuel Adams (at right) thought that America should become an independent nation.

new British land was covered by a carpet of trackless forest inhabited by Indian tribes. Here and there, the British maintained an isolated fort. The thirteen colonies — New Hampshire, Massachusetts, Rhode Island, Connecticut, New York, New Jersey, Pennsylvania, Delaware, Maryland, Virginia, North Carolina, South Carolina, and Georgia — were strung out in a narrow belt that ran almost the whole length of the Atlantic seacoast.

These colonies were prosperous, and were becoming more so with each passing year. Rich farmland was available to any man who had the ambition to clear it. In New England, craftsmen were turning out fine furniture and cabinet work, silverware, soap, candles, leather goods, guns, gunpowder, and sailing ships for the rapidly increasing trade with England. The big merchants were becoming wealthy.

In the South, the owners of great plantations, using slave labor, were harvesting shipload after shipload of to-

Shiploads of tobacco were harvested by the laborers of the big plantations in the South.

bacco, rice, indigo, and cotton, that were sent to the mother country.

Cities sprang up — Boston, New York, and Philadelphia in the North; Williamsburg, Norfolk, and Charleston in the South. Schooners plied on fairly regular schedules between the colonies. Cleared roads replaced the blazed trails of earlier days. Inns and taverns began to appear along the main highways, assuring travelers of a hot meal and a night's lodging. Guidebooks appeared that indicated the best routes between the larger towns.

Mail routes and stage lines were organized. A stagecoach called the "Flying Machine" made the trip between New York and Philadelphia in two days. The journey between New York and Boston required four or five days.

Every city had one or more newspapers, and these were distributed to outlying villages and towns. Most of the colonists of the upper and middle classes could read. Through the newspapers, the people of one colony could learn what was happening in other col-

onies. A sense of American nationalism began to develop.

Most colonists considered themselves Englishmen and loyal subjects of the King. At this time, only a few colonists, among them the firebrand Sam Adams, had ideas of America becoming an independent nation. Still, the colonists realized that they were different from their English cousins in the old country — in their customs, their way of life, and even in their language. And they called themselves Americans.

These Americans added their own words to the English language, such as *fall* (for autumn), *skunk, hickory, swap, coldsnap, handy, and Yankee.* Outside of the cities, the Americans lived a hard and adventurous life, as opposed to the drab routine existence of the average Englishman back home.

Whether the Americans realized it or not, the seeds of revolution and independence were slowly being planted. The government of the King, across the sea in London, blindly watered these seeds and helped them grow.

The cost of the French and Indian war had tremendously drained the British treasury. It more than doubled Great Britain's national debt. The yearly budget for maintaining British troops and civil officials in the American colonies had soared five hundred percent. The British government felt that, in all fairness, the colonists should bear their share of this financial burden.

Very few leaders in America could argue with this point of view. Unfortunately, King George and his ministers levied and enforced these new taxes in a high-handed way, infuriating the rugged colonists.

The English parliamentary leaders persisted in thinking of the American colonies merely as possessions that should remain permanently inferior to England. They felt that the colonies existed only to provide the motherland with abundant supplies of rice, cotton, indigo, and sugar, and to buy British manufactured goods at sky-high prices. This one-sided opinion ignored the more liberal arguments in favor of the colonists as put forth by two other Englishmen, William Pitt and Edmund Burke, and eventually resulted in the Americans' fight for independence.

Shortly after the end of the French and Indian War, the British Parliament began to pass a series of tax and trade laws that severely damaged the colonial economy. Colonial leaders protested that they should be allowed to pass their own tax laws, or at least be repre-

sented in Parliament. To these requests King George III turned a deaf ear. After the passing of the Quartering Act and the Stamp Act (1765), the first war cry of the coming revolution was heard: "Taxation without representation is tyranny!"

The Quartering Act, one of the most difficult laws for the colonists to accept, provided that Americans should support a British army of occupation stationed in the colonies to enforce the tax laws. American citizens were obliged to take Redcoat soldiers into their own homes, and provide them with food and lodging. In Boston and in other cities, resentment against these unwelcome guests led directly to the first bloodshed of the Revolution.

On the evening of March 5, 1770, a

THE BOSTON MASSACRE

What was the result of the 'Tea Act?'

On December 16, 1773, the next dramatic incident took place that led the outraged colonists one more step toward war. This was known as the Boston Tea Party. The Townshend Acts (1767), unlike the Stamp and Quartering Acts, had levied a tax on imported goods. But after an American boycott, these Acts were repealed in 1770, except for the tax on tea. This enabled the English East India Company to sell tea in the colonies more cheaply than American wholesalers could. The American merchants had been bypassed and were enraged.

When three English ships loaded with tea docked in Boston Harbor, a group of men disguised as Indians forced their way on board, tore open the hatches, and dumped the cargo of tea into the water. As they were doing this, thousands of people stood on the dock and cheered.

crowd of Boston people were shouting insults at a squad of British soldiers. Small boys began to throw snowballs, and one sentry was struck by a club. Captain Preston, a British officer, brought several men to the sentry's assistance. Suddenly the soldiers turned and fired their muskets into the crowd, killing four men and wounding several others. The country was horrified at what it called the "Boston Massacre."

During what later became known as the Boston Tea Party, American patriots dressed as Indians dumped chests of tea into the Boston harbor, while a huge crowd cheered on the wharf.

The Revolution Begins

The British government tried to punish the colonists for the tea incident by passing the "Intolerable Acts" (1774), which closed the port of Boston. But these acts only served to unite the colonists. They met at the First Continental Congress in Philadelphia in 1774 to discuss their grievances. The movement for full independence was under way, spurred on by Patrick Henry's famous cry: "I know not what course others may take; but as for me, give me liberty or give me death!"

In the months that followed, anti-British feeling in the colonies became more and more widespread. When the British ignored the pleas of the Congress, militia units were organized in every Massachusetts town. Volunteers called themselves Minute Men, because they said they were ready to take up arms "at a minute's notice" to protect their freedom. These militia companies began to hide secret stores of guns and ammunition in various places in case they would have to fight.

Early in April of 1775, General Thomas Gage, the British commander in Boston, learned from spies that such a store of war material had been hidden in the nearby town of Concord. He planned to march his army on a secret raid to capture the supplies early in the morning of April 19.

But the colonials, who had more spies in Boston than General Gage had throughout the countryside, quickly learned of his scheme. They planned that when the British army began to march, church bells in all the surrounding towns would ring to summon the Minute Men to the defense of Concord.

Paul Revere, a Boston silversmith who had become famous as a Colonial dispatch rider, was chosen to ride and spread the alarm when the British began their march. Fearing that he might be captured before he left the closely guarded city, he made plans to send a signal to other riders across the river in Charlestown. If the British army were marching by land across Boston Neck, Revere was to hang one lantern in the tower of the Old North Church. If they were going by water over the Charles River, he would hang two lanterns.

At about ten o'clock on the night of April 18, Revere received word that the British were going to leave Boston by the water route. Accordingly, he had a friend hang two lanterns in the church tower, and then he set out by boat for Charlestown. In his famous poem, "The Midnight Ride of Paul Revere," Henry Wadsworth Longfellow confused the matter of the lantern signals, and so he has misled four generations of school children. Longfellow said that the lanterns were a signal *to* Revere. Actually they were a signal *from* him.

As an added precaution, Paul Revere sent another rider, a young man named William Dawes, to Concord by

Minute Men kept the British army under fire every step of the way from Concord to Boston.

way of Boston Neck. Although they had narrow scrapes with British patrols, both riders made it as far as the town of Lexington, about ten miles from Concord. Here the two met, halted briefly to rest their horses, and refreshed themselves with a mug of hot buttered rum at Buckman's Tavern. At Buckman's, they picked up a third rider, young Doctor Sam Prescott, who volunteered to go the rest of the way with them.

Midway between Lexington and Concord, the three were ambushed by a British patrol. Revere and Dawes were captured, but Prescott made it to Concord with the warning.

When the British army marched into Lexington, they were met on the Village Green by a small force of Minute Men. Ordered to disperse by the British commander, the Colonials refused. Someone fired a shot. Nobody knows from which side it came, but general shooting then began. When the smoke of battle cleared away, eight dead Americans lay on the grass. The rest of the Colonials had retreated into the surrounding woods and fields. The British marched on toward Concord.

At famed Concord Bridge, they met a determined band of several hundred Minute Men who had been summoned by the clanging churchbells. Ralph Waldo Emerson immortalized the scene in verse:

Ethan Allen ferries his Green Mountain Boys over Lake Champlain in a surprise attack on Fort Ticonderoga.

*"By the rude bridge that arched the flood,
Their flag to April's breeze unfurled,
Here once the embattled farmers stood
And fired the shot heard round the world."*

Outnumbered and taken by surprise, it was the Britishers' turn to run. As they retreated down the narrow road back to Boston, the army was kept under fire every step of the way by Minute Men who were shooting from behind trees, barns, rail fences and stone walls. Had the Colonial army been made up of frontiersmen with deadly accurate rifles, instead of farmers with clumsy old-fashioned muskets, it is doubtful that a single Redcoat would have survived.

The Redcoats halted sometimes, and returned the fire in volleys that were mostly wasted on empty air. They finally reached Boston in the evening, with 273 Britishers lost in battle.

Thus, the first battle of the Revolutionary War ended in a rousing victory for the Yankees, and humiliation for the proud army of General Gage.

Ticonderoga and Crown Point

Who led the
Green Mountain Boys
to victory?

When news of the battles of Lexington and Concord was flashed throughout all the colonies by special messengers, the bonds of loyalty that held Americans to the crown became stretched to the breaking point. The war was on! Minute Men by the thousands poured into Cambridge, across the river from Boston. Volunteer companies were formed as far south as South Carolina. Boston, garrisoned by some 5,000 soldiers, virtually became a city under seige. All supplies from the surrounding countryside were cut off by the Yankee volunteers.

Ethan Allen, a commander of a Vermont militia company called the Green Mountain Boys, led the next offensive move. Two forts on Lake Champlain, in upper New York state, were used chiefly as ammunition depots by the British. Since they were in such a remote location, both were lightly guarded. Allen determined to capture them and carry off the supplies.

He marched his men over the mountains to the lake, seized as many boats as he could and, on the night of May 10, 1775, fell upon Ticonderoga and captured its surprised garrison without a fight. Two days later, the Green Mountain Boys took Crown Point. They then transported the muskets, powder and ball to the Colonial army outside of Boston. During the following winter, when snow lay heavy on the ground, the big guns from the forts were dragged across the rugged mountains in what was one of the greatest engineering feats of the war.

Bunker Hill

In June, 1775, the Second Continental Congress adopted the growing, but poorly organized New England Army. They appointed George Washington commanding general.

A volunteer army of more than 20,000 Yankees surrounded Boston on every side. Inside the city, a veteran army of 6,000 or 7,000 well-trained British troops were virtually prisoners. The British were well equipped, but their food supplies were running low. As they looked at the hordes of Americans all around them, the men became restless and eager for some sort of showdown. The British officers, Generals Gage, Howe, Clinton and Burgoyne, felt the same way.

The scene was set for an epic battle that was one of the decisive turning

GENERAL ISRAEL PUTNAM

points of the Revolutionary War. After the battle ended, colonists no longer doubted that the American colonies must break all ties with Great Britain.

In Boston, the beseiged British had decided to occupy and fortify the hills on the Charlestown peninsula directly across the harbor from Boston. But the

Americans heard of the plan, and on the night of June 16, 1775, landed on the peninsula, bypassed Bunker Hill and took Breed's Hill, which was nearer Boston. During the night, Colonel William Prescott had led his regiment to the hilltop and had hastily thrown up some makeshift fortifications from which cannon shells might easily be lobbed into Boston itself.

As soon as there was enough light to see, a British warship in the harbor and British artillery on several hills in Boston opened fire. The bombarding, however, did little damage. Colonel Prescott's force was soon joined by officers and men from a number of other Yankee units. Among these officers was General Israel Putnam, a veteran of the French and Indian War. When he heard the news of Lexington and Concord, he had come out of retirement and offered his services. Working alongside the men, General Putnam directed the hasty building of more fortifications.

In Boston, the British high command held an immediate council of war. The decision was made to attack as quickly as possible with a frontal assault on the hill. Command of the attacking force was given to General Howe. He at once began to ferry his men across the harbor to Charlestown.

Even after the costly lesson of the retreat from Concord, the British regulars had nothing but contempt for colonial militia. Now, dressed in full uniform and carrying heavy packs that weighed nearly one hundred pounds per man, they climbed over stone walls, struggled through plowed fields, and advanced up the slope as well as they

The battle at Bunker Hill was bloody. The Americans retreated only after their ammunition ran out.

could in precise formation. Realizing that his men were low in powder and cannon balls, Colonel Prescott cautioned them to hold their fire until the oncoming ranks were in range. "Wait until you see the whites of their eyes!" he ordered.

The gleaming white cross belts of the British made perfect targets. When the order was given to fire, their ranks were mowed down before the Yankee guns like ripe grain before a scythe. Such punishment was more than the advancing soldiers could take. The Redcoats retreated out of musket range.

Once again they formed their lines at the base of the hill. Once again they advanced against the Yankees. Once again they ran up against a deadly stone wall of murderous lead. And for the second time, they retreated in bloody confusion, leaving the slopes littered with the bright uniforms of their fallen comrades.

More reinforcements came from Boston, and General Howe ordered a third attempt on the hill. Again the slaughter continued. Then suddenly the Yankee firing stopped. The defenders of the hill had completely run out of ammunition. They quickly retreated from the hill and went back to the mainland, leaving Bunker and Breed's Hill in possession of the remainder of the British army.

Some fifteen hundred Redcoats had been killed or wounded in the brief, but bloody engagement. The American dead were one hundred and forty; the wounded two hundred and seventy-one.

Once again the British generals learned to their sorrow that the American "rabble in arms," as Burgoyne called them, could fight as long as they were supplied with powder and ball.

George Washington, Commander-in-Chief of the Continental Army, hurried at once to Cambridge. He arrived on July 2, but found supplies so scarce, and discipline in the militia ranks so lax, that he spent the next eight months trying to whip his army into fighting shape. All summer, fall and winter, Washington worked to turn the volunteers into an efficient fighting force. In the spring of 1776, he decided to drive the British once and for all out of Boston.

Amazingly enough, the British General Howe, who had succeeded Gage as supreme commander, had neglected to fortify the Dorchester Hills that overlooked Boston from the south. Washington now proceeded to fortify them, putting the British army in Boston at the mercy of his guns. There was nothing for the British to do but evacuate the city.

Although no formal agreement was made, both sides understood that Washington's men would not molest the British while they embarked, if the British in turn, left Boston without damaging the city. Thus, on March 17, General Howe's army sailed out of the port of Boston for Halifax, taking with them about one thousand colonists who were still loyal to the king.

Benedict Arnold at Quebec

While these stirring events were going on around Boston, a brash young officer of the Connecticut militia named Benedict Arnold, conceived the idea of a bold attack on the fortress city of Quebec, in Canada. An invasion of Canada, via Lake Champlain and Montreal, was already under way, led by General Richard Montgomery. Arnold proposed to General Washington that he lead an army north through the wilderness of Maine, join up with Montgomery, and surround Quebec.

Since the capture of Quebec would cut off the British northern source of supplies that came through the St. Lawrence River, Washington gave his consent. Arnold at once set out to recruit an army in Maine, New Hampshire and Vermont.

The march of Arnold's men is a classic in military history. In one of the worst New England autumns in years, he started up the Kennebec River with an army of eleven hundred men. They carried their supplies in crude flatboats called bateaux. Cold, snow and freezing rain dogged them every mile of the miserable way. Dozens of Arnold's followers died of exposure. But he relentlessly continued.

Just south of Moosehead Lake in late

General Montgomery's men followed the rocky trail around Cape Diamond until they were halted by salvos of cannon fire.

October, the expedition moved westward, across the Chain of Ponds, to Lake Megantic and the headwaters of the Chaudière River. From here they floated down to the St. Lawrence River and Quebec.

For a month after arriving at the St. Lawrence, Arnold rested his weary men and waited for Montgomery, who had taken Montreal and was moving to join Arnold's forces. On New Year's Eve, 1775, in a blinding snowstorm, the two armies made a desperate effort to scale the sheer rock walls upon which the city of Quebec was built. Montgomery was killed, and Arnold was wounded in the knee. After a stiff fight, the Americans were forced to withdraw, but they kept a tight blockade on the city for the balance of the winter.

With the coming of British reinforcements in the spring, Arnold was forced to retreat by way of Montreal and Lake Champlain. He was pursued by General Guy Carleton, who intended to defeat him and then capture upper New York state. When Arnold turned on his pursuer at the Battle of Valcour Island and whipped him soundly, Carlton returned to Canada and New York was saved.

Why did Benedict Arnold turn traitor?

Because of his spectacular march on Quebec, his victory at Valcour Island, and the important part he later played in winning the Battle of Saratoga, Benedict Arnold was soon one of the popular heroes of the Revolution. But, being an extremely vain man, he was offended when he was passed over for promotion. Furthermore, he had extravagant tastes, and was constantly in financial trouble. When he found that he could sell military secrets to the British for large sums of money, his patriotism gave way to greed.

In 1780, while in command of West Point, he arranged to surrender it for twenty thousand pounds. When this plan was discovered, Arnold fled to the British lines. He was made a brigadier in the British army; but the British had no more use for a traitor than did the Americans.

Arnold died in disgrace in England in 1801. History will always remember him, not for his deeds of valour, but for his acts of treachery.

What was the Olive Branch Petition?

The Declaration of Independence

After the bloody battles at Lexington and Concord, the enthusiasm for independence was further stimulated by Thomas Paine's stirring pamphlet, *Common Sense*. He wrote, "These are the times that try men's souls. The summer soldier and the sunshine patriot will, in this crisis shrink from the service of their country.... Tyranny, like hell, is not easily conquered." Washington had the pamphlet read aloud to his soldiers, and more than 100,000 copies were sold.

The American Congress still made one last attempt toward reconciliation by sending a final petition to King George. Called the Olive Branch Petition, it sought once again some way by which England and her American colonies could find a solution to their mutual problems.

The King's reaction was one of contempt. He at once declared that the colonies were in a state of armed rebellion; and parliament followed this with a new act forbidding all trade with the thirteen colonies.

The Americans desperately needed war supplies. But by now the leaders in Congress realized that no foreign nation would trade with them as long as they considered themselves subjects of Great Britain. It was clear that the only hope of securing foreign aid lay in declaring the American colonies a free and independent nation.

Who was responsible for the famous declaration?

In early June, Congress appointed a committee to draw up such a declaration. Two of the members were Thomas Jefferson and Benjamin Franklin. The committee agreed on the main points to be covered, and then turned the actual writing of the document over to Jefferson. After a number of changes and revisions had been made in Jefferson's original draft, the Second Continental Congress formally adopted the Declaration on July 4, 1776. By the end of the summer, it had been officially adopted by each of the thirteen colonies that now composed the infant United States of America.

Independence Day, John Adams prophesied, would be "celebrated by succeeding generations as the great anniversary festival. It ought to be solemnized with pomp and parade, with shows, games, sports, guns, bells, bonfires, and

After agreement was reached concerning the main points of the document, the actual writing of the Declaration of Independence was done by Thomas Jefferson.

19

illuminations, from one end of the continent to the other, from this time forward, forevermore."

And, as we all know, it has been and always will be.

> **What basic principles are expressed in the Declaration?**

Historians generally consider the Declaration of Independence to be one of the greatest human documents of all time. In ringing phrases it sets forth a philosophy of government that had never been voiced, a statement of basic principles that no oppressed people had ever dared to say out loud.

It declares three basic truths:

"That all men are created equal; that they are endowed by their Creator with certain unalienable rights; that among these are Life, Liberty, and the Pursuit of Happiness."

"That governments derive their just powers from the consent of the governed."

"That when any form of government becomes destructive of these ends, it is the right of the people to alter or abolish it and to institute a new government."

These simple truths ignited a flame that was soon to spread like wildfire around the world. They sparked the French Revolution, and the revolt of the South American countries against the Spanish and Portuguese kings. Today their echoes can still be heard in the struggles for freedom among the new nations of Africa and Asia.

Now, with the Declaration of Independence at last adopted, the die was cast. There could be no turning back, even in the unlikely event that the king and parliament might decide to change their minds and come to terms. The war had to be won decisively. The British army had to be driven from American shores. Failure was unthinkable. As old Ben Franklin put it so pointedly when he affixed his signature to the Declaration: "Now, gentlemen, we must hang together. Or, assuredly, we will all hang separately." But it was going to be a long up-hill fight, and no one knew it better than George Washington.

> **Why were the Hessians enlisted?**

The British Army and the Yankee Army

The British army in America in 1776 and 1777 was a formidable fighting force, as reckoned by standards of that day. This army consisted of the nine thousand men that General Howe had evacuated from Boston. More Redcoats were detached from service in Ireland and transferred to North America. Convicted criminals from English jails were offered the choice of army service or imprisonment.

King George, realizing that he

needed a larger army, hired thirty thousand German soldiers and shipped them to the colonies. Because most of them came from one German state, Hesse-Cassel, these soldiers were commonly known as Hessians.

The Hessians were good troops, well drilled and well disciplined. But who could expect them to fight very hard? They had nothing for which to fight. Many of these Germans deserted to the American side, accepted homesteads, and subsequently became successful farmers and loyal American citizens.

Several thousand loyalist Americans who were opposed to independence, fought for the British king. The most famous of these loyalist regiments was Tarleton's Legion.

The British leaders also sought to enlist Indian tribes to fight against the colonists. For the most part, the Indians hated the colonists because the frontiersmen had invaded their hunting grounds. The British promised that these hunting grounds would be left alone if King George won the war. The Indians harassed frontier settlements. But as reliable fighting men, they were of little or no use. Whenever endangered, they melted away into the forest and disappeared.

Who were the "Citizen Soldiers?"

George Washington never knew from one day to the next exactly how many men he had in his army. In the first burst of patriotic outrage after Lexington and Concord, some twenty to thirty thousand men volunteered for military duty. But this number rapidly diminished as these "citizen soldiers" returned to their farms to plant or harvest their crops.

Nearly all of the American soldiers were members of state militia units and had volunteered for only a few weeks at a time. When the periods of their enlistments expired, they simply shouldered their muskets and drifted away.

As an ex-officer of the British army, Washington dreamed of putting together a regular, well trained American military force. To encourage volunteers, large bounties were offered, including promises of free farmland at the war's end. But the regular Colonial Army never exceeded more than five or six thousand men.

On the other hand, the militiamen were always ready to turn out for a few weeks to meet emergencies. The knowledge that they would always be met by large masses of untrained, but determined farmers, kept the British constantly off balance.

British deserters made a small but steady contribution to Washington's army. These men, most of whom could never hope to own property in the old country, were lured by the prospect of free land in the New World, and of a future life in a free country.

Thus, George Washington proposed to win the independence of the new United States with a makeshift army. It was poorly equipped, poorly clothed, and poorly fed. It was outnumbered and outgunned in almost every engagement it fought. It was led by officers who, for the most part, had little or no military training. It was chiefly by a series of lucky breaks, and British blunders, that the American army managed to win in the end.

Under the cover of a driving rainstorm, a regiment of ex-fishermen from Salem and Marblehead rowed the entire army of General Washington across the East River to the temporary safety of Manhattan.

What was General Howe's next target?

The Campaign in New York

After the British commander General William Howe had evacuated his army from Boston in the spring of 1776 and taken it to Halifax, he immediately had set about building it into the biggest fighting force yet seen in America. By June, with the addition of fresh Hessian troops, he had more than 30,000 men, supported by large units of the Royal Navy.

There was little or no question about where Howe would strike next. Almost certainly his objective would be New York City. There were two major reasons for this. In the first place, New York was situated on an island surrounded by navigable water. Its main harbor was the largest in the New World. It would provide the perfect base for England's mighty fleet, and that fleet could protect it on all sides. New York would also be an ideal headquarters for the British army.

Secondly, New York commanded the mouth of the Hudson River. The Hudson leads north to Lake Champlain and Lake George, which are connected by a system of rivers with the St. Lawr-

ence and Canada. If the British could capture and control this water route, they could cut the American colonies into two halves, and conquer them one at a time. On paper, the plan looked good.

It was not difficult for George Washington to guess what was in Howe's mind. Therefore, as soon as the British had left Boston in American hands, he moved his army to New York. There he began to fortify the city, as well as the hills in Brooklyn across the East River. When Howe made his move, in late August, Washington was waiting for him on Brooklyn Heights.

The battle that ensued was a severe defeat for the Yankees. Outnumbered by about three to one and led by officers who did not know the terrain, they were at last forced to retreat. Nearly a thousand men, most of them taken as prisoners, were lost.

Now General Howe obligingly made a tactical blunder that saved the rest of Washington's army. Instead of pressing his advantage, he halted his men in front of the last Yankee line of defense, and sat there for two days.

Meanwhile a violent rainstorm had come roaring down out of the north. Under the protective cover of its driving fury, Washington collected a fleet of several hundred small boats. He put this little flotilla under charge of a regiment of ex-fishermen from Salem and

General Washington, tired and dejected, after failing to control his fleeing army on Manhattan Island.

Marblehead, Massachusetts. As the rain hammered down, these Massachusetts men rowed the entire army across the East River to the temporary safety of Manhattan.

Why was Manhattan vulnerable?

But safety of Washington's army in New York was only very temporary indeed. The British fleet could, and on several occasions did, sail around Manhattan Island unopposed. This meant that British troops could land anywhere on the island and completely cut off New York City, which was then only a small town on Manhattan's lower tip.

New York was entirely undefensible, and no one knew it better than George Washington. He at once made preparations to retreat northward to the mainland of Westchester County.

The army began the evacuation of Manhattan on September 12, taking with them their ammunition and supplies, their sick and wounded. But there was a shortage of horses and wagons, and progress northward up the island was agonizingly slow.

Then, on September 15, General Howe's troops invaded the island from Brooklyn. British warships in the East River opened up with a tremendous barrage that terrified the raw American troops and sent them fleeing northward in panic. Under cover of the gunfire, the British troops began to come ashore from landing barges. The British soldiers, immaculate in their brilliant red uniforms, pursued the fleeing Americans with parade ground precision.

When he heard the sound of the cannon fire, General Washington and his staff rode south from their temporary headquarters in Harlem, at the north

Mrs. Murray's tea party for General Howe and his staff. ➡

end of Manhattan. When he saw that the retreat had become a rout, the general attempted to stop it and organize a line of resistance. But it was no use. The fleeing men paid no attention. They threw aside everything that might hinder their running — guns, blankets, knapsacks, powder horns, overcoats — and bolted along the road north.

The story is told that Mrs. Robert Murray, a steadfast patriot despite the fact that her husband was a British sympathizer, gave a hastily-organized tea party for General Howe and his staff. She wanted to slow up the British advance and give the Americans more time to escape. Whether or not this gave Washington any extra time is debatable.

On the following day, General Washington managed to rally his men for a brief stand on Harlem Heights. Although the British were momentarily stopped, Washington realized that trying to hold Manhattan was a hopeless task. He left a garrison of some three thousand men at Fort Washington, on the Manhattan side of the Hudson, and retreated into Westchester.

Howe followed and, at the battle of White Plains, on October 28, won another victory. But, again, the British general failed to follow up his advantage and Washington was able to take his men across the Hudson River into New Jersey.

Three weeks later, Fort Washington was attacked by an overwhelming force of Hessians and every man in the fort was either killed or captured. Now all of New York was in British hands, and the remnants of Washington's army were adrift in the hills of New Jersey and Pennsylvania.

Crossing the Delaware

By Christmas of 1776, George Washington's army was all but beaten. Discouraged by an endless series of defeats and retreats westward from New York, the army had finally made camp on the Pennsylvania bank of the Delaware River, just across from the town of Trenton, New Jersey.

In the era of the Revolutionary War, it was traditional that wars were more or less called off during the winter months. Thus, General Howe had taken the main part of his army back to New York to wait for spring. He had, however, left small garrisons in a number of New Jersey towns. One of these towns was Trenton, which was held by three regiments of Hessians.

Washington decided that this was the time to strike a decisive blow, more for the sake of his army's morale than for any hope of a victory that might change the course of the war. He ordered every boat for miles up and down the river to be assembled for an attack. It was to be an all-or-nothing try. His army had only a slim chance to get back across the river if the attack failed. But Washington was willing to gamble.

Christmas night, 1776, was bitterly cold. The Delaware River was filled with large, floating chunks of ice, and the air was a swirl of sleet. Washington's men were dressed in flimsy summer clothes, and most of them wore no boots. Their feet were wrapped in rags for protection against the biting cold. Their footprints left bloody tracks in the snow.

At daybreak, the Americans landed on the Trenton side of the river and charged into the town. Most of the Hessians had been up all night, drinking wine and celebrating the holiday. Before they had time to come to their senses, they were surrounded. Their commander, Colonel Rall, was killed. The entire garrison of about a thousand men was captured.

News of Washington's victory lifted the spirits of all the American colonists, and then another victory followed on its heels.

General Charles Cornwallis, who was later to surrender at Yorktown in the final battle that won the war for Washington's army, marched south from his headquarters in Princeton in an attempt to recapture Trenton. Washington lured him on by keeping the

Yankee campfires burning; but meanwhile he took the bulk of his army in a surprise march around the British rear. Almost before he knew what was happening, Cornwallis found himself surrounded by shooting, shouting Americans. He retreated toward Trenton, but the rear guard of his army, which had fallen back toward Princeton, was taken prisoner.

Brandywine and Germantown

Why did General Howe take his men to sea?

After his surprise victories at Trenton and Princeton, Washington took his army into winter quarters at Morristown, N. J. Actually, he went with what remained of his army, for most enlistments were up at the end of 1776. Once more the general was faced with the heartbreaking task of signing up new men.

Washington feared that Howe might attack while he was in the process of forming a new army. But once again General Howe obliged. He kept his army in New York.

Things remained quiet on the New Jersey front until the end of July. By this time, Washington had managed to put together an army of about 8,000 men. Howe then pulled a surprise move by embarking his entire force of 17,000 on a huge fleet of transports and putting out to sea.

Where was Howe going? Washington sweated out the answer to that question for a month. Then the British army began to make landings on the northern shore of Chesapeake Bay in Maryland, and marched toward Philadelphia, the capital of the United States. Washington quickly moved his men south to head off the British.

The two armies met at the violent battle of Brandywine Creek, and once again the Americans were outmaneuvered, if not outfought, and badly beaten. Howe captured Philadelphia,

The British were able to surprise General Anthony Wayne and his troops encamped at Paoli, near Philadelphia. Using only bayonets, the British lost only a few, but killed or wounded many Americans.

Colonel Henry Knox, making a mistake that proved to be costly, orders his men to level Chew Mansion with cannon fire.

Below, a portrait of General Anthony Wayne, who, for his bravery and courage was nicknamed "Mad Anthony."

and the Continental Congress fled to the town of York, Pennsylvania.

Now Washington planned another surprise attack on the British, this time at their headquarters in the village of Germantown just outside Philadelphia. The battle began well for the Yankees. They closed in on the British from four sides. Then an American officer made a fatal mistake.

About a hundred Redcoats had taken refuge in the Chew Mansion, a large stone house, and opened fire on the oncoming Americans. Instead of going around the house and keeping it behind them, the Yankee commander, Colonel Henry Knox, ordered his men to level the house with cannon fire.

The sudden cannonading and the clouds of powder smoke only served to confuse the advancing Americans. By the time they were able to reorganize, their ammunition was exhausted, and they were forced to retreat.

General Howe now held one of the most important American cities. He and his troops spent a comfortable winter in Philadelphia. Meanwhile, British supplies could be shipped up the Delaware River.

Once again, Washington moved his army into quarters for the winter, this time in Valley Forge, Pennsylvania.

Valley Forge

The winter of 1777-78, which Washington and his men spent encamped at Valley Forge, was one of the most miserable experiences that any army in history ever had to endure. The weather was unusually bitter and cold, and the snow was unusually deep. The men were ragged. Very few had shoes. As they had done at Trenton the winter before, they wrapped their feet in old rags for protection, and again left bloody tracks wherever they walked.

Those among the men who had enough clothes to work outdoors, cut down trees to make shacks and lean-tos. There were no horses, and the men pulled their own home-made sleds over the snow.

Worst of all, the soldiers were half-starved, an inexcusable situation because many farmers in that part of Pennsylvania had stores of meat and grain in their smokehouses and corn-cribs. But they refused to take American paper dollars in exchange for it, and Washington had no gold or silver. Even if farmers would sell some produce, there was no way to transport it safely.

The Continental Congress, then in session in York, Pennsylvania, could do little to alleviate Washington's dire plight. This Congress had no power to tax people or goods. The only way for them to raise money was to borrow it. Congress went deeper and deeper into debt, and these debts could never be

Martha Washington visits her husband.

repaid unless the colonies won the war. So they were reluctant to send money if they could not see a quick victory.

But George Washington was determined to keep his little army together, and he stayed with his men at Valley Forge and shared their hardships. Hundreds of his soldiers left when their enlistment terms expired. Others, half starved and half frozen, simply walked off through the woods and went home.

Some of Washington's ragged soldiers inside a primitive log hut at Valley Forge.

But those who had the courage and determination to stick with their commander, became the hard core of a new American army that was finally to go on and win the war.

Toward the end of the winter, Washington was joined by an unexpected recruit. This was Baron Friedrich von Steuben, a professional German officer who had served under Frederick the Great.

The American soldiers, even though

Washington meets von Steuben, who volunteered to teach the troops drilling and maneuvering principles.

they had been through many battles, had never had any basic military training. Von Steuben now became their drill master. He taught them how to march in military formation, how to handle their guns properly, how to exe-

cute commands, and, in general, how to conduct themselves like soldiers.

When they next went into action, at the battle of Monmouth in the following June, they showed that von Steuben's training had paid off. They stood up to the best the British had to offer, and finally won the day.

Who instigated the Conway Cabal?

As if Washington did not have enough to worry about at Valley Forge, a conspiracy against him was brewing in the Congress. It was headed by General Horatio Gates, who was taking credit for the victory over Burgoyne at Saratoga, and General Thomas Conway, a French officer of Irish descent who was on Gates' staff. This plot was known as the Conway Cabal, cabal being an old-fashioned word for intrigue.

The plotters schemed to oust Wash-

Saratoga

While George Washington was having his major troubles and minor triumphs in New Jersey and Pennsylvania, the British war office in far-off London set the wheels of its grand strategy in motion. The object was to divide the colonies in two, and defeat one half at a time. The plan had three parts.

General John Burgoyne was to march his army of 7,500 British and Hessian regulars down from Quebec, by way of Lake Champlain. Colonel Barry St. Leger, with a well-organized force that included 1,000 Indians, would move eastward from Lake Ontario, down the Mohawk River. General Howe would bring his huge army up the Hudson from New York City. When the three armies converged at Albany, the northern half of the colonies would be firmly caught in the net.

But from the very beginning, things went wrong. For some reason, Howe did not receive his orders and, as we have seen, took his army south to Philadelphia. St. Leger's operation went smoothly until he ran up against stubborn resistance by a small group of American militia at Fort Stanwix, a wilderness outpost on the site of the present city of Rome, N. Y. Vastly outnumbered, it seemed that the defenders of the fort were doomed. The outlook became even grimmer when a party of 800 volunteers, on their way to relieve the fort, was ambushed and all but wiped out by St. Leger's Indians at Oriskany. Then Benedict Arnold did by

ington from his command of all American forces and replace him with Gates. The true reasons behind the cabal have remained obscure. But a few facts are apparent. Some officers, like Gates, were jealous of the fact that Washington was the popular hero of the people. Others felt that while Gates had been successful in the crucial battle of Saratoga, Washington's record was only a series of failures and near-failures. Some congressmen feared that Washington wanted to eventually set himself up as the king of the United States.

Washington, of course, knew what was going on. But he kept himself aloof from the controversy and devoted all his time to keeping his army together at Valley Forge. If he ever got discouraged and wanted to quit, he did not show it.

The Conway Cabal petered out in the spring, and George Washington once more went about his business of leading his fight against the British.

trickery what could not be done by force.

He sent a spy into St. Leger's camp, to tell the Indians that an overpowering American force was on its way to massacre them all. The Indians mutinied, seized St. Leger's supplies of whiskey, got drunk, and deserted into the woods. With most of his force gone, St. Leger had to give up and go back to Canada the way he had come.

Meanwhile, General Burgoyne was having his difficulties too. Known as "Gentleman Johnny," Burgoyne paid more attention to the fine clothes he wore and the fine food that he and his staff ate, than to the business of running his army. He knew nothing about fighting in the wilderness and neither did his officers.

At Bennington, Vermont, Burgoyne lost nearly 1,000 men when a raiding party, sent out to steal horses and cattle, was surprised by Yankee militiamen. A month later, on September 19, 1777, as the cumbersome British column was painfully making its way through the thick forests, it was attacked by an American force at Freeman's Farm and soundly beaten.

Another two weeks passed, while Burgoyne sat and tried to figure out what to do. Then the Americans, sparked once more by the dashing Arnold, hit again at a place called Saratoga. This time, "Gentleman Johnny" was finished. When he surrendered to General Horatio Gates, the Yankee commander, the British fighting forces in America had been dealt a staggering blow from which they never recovered. They lost seven generals, 300 lesser officers, over 5,000 men, 27 cannons, more than 5,000 muskets, as well as vast supplies of powder, ball, food and other stores. Most historians agree that Saratoga was the turning point of the Revolutionary War.

Monmouth

Who was the heroine of the Battle of Monmouth?

In the spring of 1778, General Howe resigned as commander-in-chief of the British forces. His army had spent a comfortable winter in Philadelphia while Washington's men had been freezing in Valley Forge. But Howe had become convinced that trying to subdue the American rebels was a hopeless task that could only end in failure. His place was taken by General Sir Henry Clinton.

Clinton's first order of business was to retreat from Philadelphia and take his army back to New York. When Washington learned of this movement, he decided to attack.

By June, Washington had built his strength up to some 12,000 men. Thanks to the rigorous training program of von Steuben, they were fit and combat-ready. What Washington did not know was that he had a traitor on his staff.

General Charles Lee was an ex-British officer who had joined the American cause. Because of his military background, which Lee had taken great pains to exaggerate, Washington welcomed him and made him second in

"Gentleman Johnny" surrenders to General Horatio Gates at Saratoga.

General Washington at right, relieves General Lee of his command at the Battle of Monmouth and gives Lee a severe tongue lashing in the presence of the men.

command. A year before, during the retreat across New Jersey, Lee had been captured by the British. During his term of imprisonment, Lee had decided that the Americans could not win the war and so he turned his coat again. He gave the British a detailed plan for defeating Washington.

Now, just before Washington was to attack Clinton, Lee was exchanged for an English general and returned to duty with the American army. Washington gave him back his old job as second in command. Washington's plan was to have Lee take a forward element of the army and attack Clinton's columns. When the British turned to fight, Washington would then come up with the rest of his army and finish Clinton off once and for all.

Lee made his attack, as planned, near the little town of Monmouth Court House in New Jersey. But when the British resisted, also as planned, Lee ordered a retreat instead of fighting until Washington came to reinforce him.

When Washington discovered what was going on, he galloped forward furiously, gave Lee a severe tongue lashing in the presence of the men, and ordered him off the field in disgrace.

Thanks to von Steuben's training, Washington's men fought well. But Lee's disgraceful conduct had cost the Americans precious time. Clinton managed to take his army to New York.

At the battle of Monmouth, Molly Pitcher earned her place in the history books. Her real name was Mary Hayes and she was the wife of John Hayes, one of Washington's cannoneers. At the start of the battle, she carried pitchers of fresh water to the soldiers in the fighting line. Then, when she saw her husband collapse at his gun, she dropped her pitcher and began to fire the cannon. She continued to keep the cannon firing until the battle was over.

The American Navy

What role did sea warfare play in the Revolution?

The Revolutionary War was a land war in which America's midget sea power played only a minor role. The British Navy, at the outbreak of the war, was the mightiest in the world. For this reason, the British armies had little trouble capturing and holding such seaports as New York, Charleston and Savannah. And because Britain relied so heavily on her navy for delivering supplies, her inland troops like those at Saratoga, found themselves constantly in danger of isolation from supply lines.

The most important segment of American power on the sea was her vast fleet of privateers. These privately-owned armed ships were little more than legalized pirates. Congress issued their owners "letters of marque" which gave them a legitimate right to prey on British merchant ships.

At one time or another, more than 2,000 of these privateers roamed the seas, all the way from the West Indies and the American coast, to Spain and the English Channel. When they came upon an unarmed merchantman, they put a prize crew aboard and sailed the captured ship into the nearest neutral port. Here the cargo and the ship itself were sold, and the money divided between the owner, the captain and the crews.

Many wealthy American families today owe the beginnings of their fortunes to the fact that their ancestors owned or captained Revolutionary privateers.

Insofar as the privateers created a great deal of trouble for British merchant ships, and prevented supplies from being delivered to the English troops in America, they were an asset to the American cause. But sailors much preferred the easy life on a privateer and the easy money to be made from prizes, to service with the little American Navy or the ground troops. To this extent they were an evil.

Early in the war, Congress appropriated money for a small regular navy.

COMMODORE ESEK HOPKINS

Commodore Esek Hopkins was put in command. He was a daring man, although difficult for his superiors in Congress to get along with. His little squadrons inflicted much damage on British installations throughout the West Indies.

A few states had warships of their own. The most famous of these was the Massachusetts ship, *Protector*. While cruising off the Grand Banks, in June of 1780, she met the British ship *Admiral Duff*. Both warships were about the same size, but the *Protector* was better served by her crew.

As the two ships came together,

sixty American Marines scrambled to the tops of her masts and proceeded to shoot down the crewmen in the Britisher's rigging, as well as the sailor at the helm. Meanwhile, the *Protector's* deck guns hammered at her enemy. The *Duff's* sails caught fire, and the flames quickly ran down to a powder magazine below decks. The *Duff* blew up and sank almost instantly.

When, in 1778, the French decided to come into the war as America's ally, the huge French fleet joined the side of the Yankees. The French were mainly interested in utilizing their naval power against the English in the West Indies and elsewhere. French warships did, however, transport large numbers of French soldiers to be added to Washington's army. At Yorktown, in the war's last battle, a French fleet defeated a smaller English fleet that had attempted to come to the aid of the British forces and thus contributed greatly to the final victory.

The most fabulous American ship of the war could hardly be called American at all except for the flag that flew at her masthead. She was an ex-French merchantman, her name was French, and her captain was a Scotsman. Her crew of 306 included 79 Americans and 137 French Marines. The remainder were Scotch, Irish, Scandinavians and Portuguese. Yet she became one of the most famous ships in the story of American naval history.

She was the *Bon Homme Richard*, captained by John Paul Jones. The *Bon Homme Richard* was so old and her timbers so rotten that they could hardly support her guns. The guns themselves were antiquated and only barely serviceable. The spirit of her young skipper was the strongest thing about her.

On September 23, 1779, while cruis-

The battle between the Bon Homme Richard and the Serapis.

ing off the coast of England, Captain Jones sighted a convoy of British merchantmen under the guard of a big, brand-new British frigate, the *Serapis*. Jones at once moved in to attack, while the merchantmen fled for the safety of the shore.

Cutaway view of a typical English warship, a 40 gun battleship, of Revolutionary times. You can see on the top story from left to right, the Galley, the officers' quarters, the crews' quarters, the captain's sleeping quarters, the officers' mess and the captain's cabin. On the lower stories are more crews' quarters, sail loft, magazine, sick bay, ship stores and even a stable for horses.

In the first broadside, two of the *Richard's* big guns burst, killing their crews, and the rest of the battery had to be abandoned. Now Jones had only his smaller guns. Meanwhile, the heavy guns of the *Serapis* were pounding him to pieces. There was only one hope. By an amazing feat of seamanship, Jones managed to ram his decrepit old ship into the *Serapis'* side and lash it there. Most of the *Richard's* guns were out of action. Her rotten timbers caught fire repeatedly, and the flames were put out only by the Herculean efforts of the crew.

Seeing that the American ship was in the worst kind of trouble, the English captain called out through his speaking horn:

"Do you ask for quarter? Will you surrender?"

Jones yelled back with his now-famous remark: "I have not yet begun to fight!"

Then someone on the *Richard* threw a grenade into the *Serapis'* hold and exploded a store of ammunition. With a small cannon, Jones knocked off the Britisher's mast. The sun went down, and the furious battle continued in the moonlit night. Then the British captain surrendered. Jones and what was left of his crew had hardly stepped on board the *Serapis* when the battered old *Richard* sank, bow first. But as she went down, her flag was still proudly flying.

John Paul Jones managed to limp his captured prize into the port of Texel, Holland. There, because the Dutch were neutral, the authorities took the *Serapis* away from him.

The famous battle proved little, ex-cept that a brave man never quits. It did no material good to the American cause. But it gave Americans a glowing sense of pride that one of their ships could defeat a mighty unit of the British navy. And it gave the British a new respect for the Americans' fighting ability. "Put to sea at once," the First Lord of the Admiralty implored one of his captains. "If you can take John Paul Jones, you will be as high in public esteem as if you had beaten the combined fleets of France and Spain."

| Why was Clark's March so difficult? | Vincennes |

Vincennes was a quiet little trading post and fort deep in the forests of what is now Indiana. Its people, mostly of French descent, were sympathetic to the cause of American independence, but they were far removed from the sound and fury of the war.

Then, on May 19, 1777, a British military unit from Detroit marched out of the woods and took possession of the fort in the king's name. Up until this time, the people of Vincennes were on friendly terms with the neighboring Indians. But now, since many of the western tribes were allies of the British, Indian attacks on settlers outside the fort became common.

At this point, a major of the Virginia militia, named George Rogers Clark, went to Governor Patrick Henry with a bold plan to attack the garrison at Vincennes and chase the British out of the northwest. The governor agreed,

Back to Vicennes through swamp and icy water.

MAJOR GEORGE ROGERS CLARK

and gave Clark men and supplies. After a grueling journey down the Ohio River and overland through rugged Indian country, Clark attacked the British garrison in August of 1778, and gave the town back to its people.

After Clark had organized the citizens of the town into a militia unit, he took his army back to Virginia. But he was gone only a few weeks when a second and larger British force, also from Detroit, captured Vincennes again. Now Clark had to redo all his work.

This time, weather conditions were infinitely worse than before. Winter rains and snows had flooded the entire countryside, and Clark's men had to make much of the 200 mile march sloughing through icy waters that were sometimes up to their shoulders. But if the floods were a miserable hardship to the Americans, the major also knew

that the weather gave him a decided strategic advantage. The British soldiers would be confined to the fort, and would not expect a surprise attack.

Clark and his wet and shivering men arrived in front of Vincennes on February 23, 1779, caught the British completely off their guard, and captured the fort without the loss of a single man. Clark then changed its name to Fort Patrick Henry.

By his bold action against the British at Vincennes, as well as at Kaskaskia and other western forts, Clark managed to keep the northwestern territory out of British hands and thus prevent an attack on the eastern colonies.

The Cherry Valley Massacre

Why was the fort attacked?

Cherry Valley was a little outpost village in northeastern New York State. Because of its exposed position, the American army had fortified it with a blockhouse the previous spring. It was garrisoned with a small force under the command of Colonel Ichabod Alden, a man who knew nothing about fighting Indians.

It has been pointed out that the chief value of the Indians to their British allies lay in harassing frontier settlements, and that they were of little help from a military standpoint. The Cherry Valley Massacre, on November 11, 1778, accomplished nothing for the British cause, but a good many helpless men, women and children were cruelly and needlessly slain.

On November 8, a friendly Indian came in to the fort and warned the colonel that a large force of Indians and American Loyalists were planning a raid on the town. But Colonel Alden did not take this information seriously.

Early in the morning of November

11, the raiding party, 800 strong, attacked the village. The white men were commanded by Captain Walter Butler, and the Indians by a half-breed Mohawk chief named Joseph Brant.

In the massacre that followed, thirty-two settlers, mostly women and children, were brutally killed, as well as Colonel Alden and fifteen of his men. The raiders burned the town, the fort, and the surrounding farms to the ground, and carried off all the livestock they could get their hands on. In addition, thirty or forty prisoners were taken, also mostly women and children. Later most of the prisoners were returned in exchange for members of Captain Butler's family that were in American hands.

Who was the "Swamp Fox?"

The British Attack in the South

After the battle of Monmouth, the last big engagement of the war in the North, the British changed their strategy. They decided to hold New York City, but send the bulk of their army south to attack the Carolinas and Virginia.

In the fall of 1779, a British army of some 3,000 men set sail from New York for Savannah, Georgia. Only a handful of Americans were there to resist, and the city was captured almost without a fight. The Americans retreated into South Carolina, leaving Georgia in British hands.

The conquest of the South was beginning to look so easy after the many British defeats and disappointments in the North, that Clinton determined to attack Charleston, the most important port in the Carolinas. This time he took a much larger army and General Cornwallis as his second in command. In February of 1780, Clinton's huge army of 10,000 men surrounded the city.

The American forces in Charleston, commanded by General Benjamin Lincoln, found themselves in a hopeless position. Lincoln had less than half as many men as Clinton. Entirely surrounded, with all possible avenues of escape cut off and no chance of getting outside help, Lincoln had no choice but to surrender. His whole army, along with its guns, ammunition and supplies fell into British hands. The American soldiers were released to go back to their homes on their promise never again to take up arms against the English king.

The British army spread out and established posts all through the state. Clinton returned to New York, leaving Cornwallis in charge.

In the British army, there were a great many Tories or Loyalists, as the

Francis Marion, the "Swamp Fox," and his guerilla forces became the terror of the English commanders.

Marion and his men, at the right in the picture, are about to ambush an enemy force.

Americans who remained loyal to the king were called. The sight of these fellow Americans strutting around proudly in redcoat uniforms was too much for the Carolina militiamen who had been paroled at the Charleston surrender. Many Americans broke their oaths and joined parties of partisan raiders under leaders like the famous Francis Marion.

Known as the "Swamp Fox," Marion was one of the great leaders of the Revolution. He and his men made their headquarters in the swamps and woods, ambushing isolated parties of British soldiers and in general making themselves the terrors of the English commanders. His scouts kept close watch on all British movements, and dashed out to strike quick and telling blows when the enemy least expected them.

Meanwhile, before the Charleston surrender, Washington had sent an army under Generals Gates and de Kalb to assist Lincoln. When he received news of the surrender, Gates determined to continue on to Camden, South Carolina. When this army finally arrived at Camden after a long and weary march through the southern woods and swamps, they found a British army waiting for them. At the first British charge, Gates' inexperienced militia threw down their guns and took to their heels. Gates, who had the fastest horse in the army, fled ahead of them in panic. General de Kalb stayed to fight and to die from eleven bullet wounds.

Two American armies had been lost in South Carolina, Lincoln's at Charleston and Gates' at Camden. Aside from such irregulars as Marion's men, there were no more American fighters in the South.

Washington recalled Gates in disgrace, and appointed a man who was his best General, Nathanael Greene, to reorganize the Southern forces.

Above, a gathering of the Mountain Men in Tennessee. At right, a scene from the battle at King's Mountain.

King's Mountain and Cowpens

An American Tory, Major Patrick Ferguson, had organized several thousand of his fellow Tories into a strong British army in North Carolina. He used them to terrorize all that part of the South by raiding and burning rebel farms, and hanging people whom he suspected of being loyal Americans. As a result, Ferguson was widely hated.

One group that was a thorn in Ferguson's side was a band of patriotic frontiersmen from the Watauga River in Tennessee. They called themselves the Watauga Men, and were all dead shots with their long rifles. Wherever and whenever they could, these men resisted the British occupation. Ferguson declared that he was going across the mountains to teach the Watauga Men a lesson.

When they heard this, the Watauga Men made up their minds that they would hit Ferguson first. Accordingly, they marched through the forests and cornered Ferguson and his men at the top of King's Mountain on the border between North and South Carolina.

All the Watauga sharpshooters climbed into trees, or fought from behind them, and picked off the Tories one by one, including Major Ferguson, himself.

At last the remaining Tories, about 700 of them, surrendered. Having put an end to Ferguson's force, the Watauga Men went back home to their farms. Thus a band of untrained mountaineers were able to hand the well trained British forces their first defeat in the South.

MAJOR GENERAL
NATHANAEL GREENE

How did Greene win at Cowpens?

Nathanael Greene, sent by Washington to replace the cowardly Gates, moved south with a mere handful of poorly equipped men. Desperately needing time to reinforce and re-equip his little army, Greene took a chance and divided it into two parts. He commanded one, and Daniel Morgan, the famous leader of the riflemen, commanded the other. Then the two divisions went their separate ways.

Cornwallis sent Tarleton to deal with Morgan. They fought at a place called Cowpens in South Carolina. Morgan adopted the same tactics as had the Watauga Men at King's Mountain. He stationed his sharpshooters in trees and behind logs, and was ready when Tarleton's army came on the scene.

Tarleton ordered a cavalry charge to dislodge the rebels, the worst possible move he could have made. The riflemen cooly shot the mounted targets. In the furious fight that followed, Tarleton lost ninety percent of his men, but he himself managed to escape.

For the second time in the South, Americans fighting "Indian style" had annihilated trained British soldiers.

45

Yorktown

For the next four months, General Greene harassed Cornwallis all up and down North Carolina. Aside from one big battle at Guilford Courthouse that Cornwallis won, but in which he lost about one-fourth of his army, the engagements were small ones. Sometimes the British were defeated, sometimes the Americans. But the effect reduced Cornwallis' army to only a shell of what it had been in early spring.

Now the scene was set for the amazing and unexpected series of events that led to the final battle of the Revolutionary War and ultimate American victory. Cornwallis left the Carolinas and moved north to Virginia. There he began a campaign of raiding and burning Virginia farms and storehouses.

Meanwhile, Washington had been keeping the main part of his army just outside of New York, waiting for a chance to strike at General Clinton who was maintaining a 15,000 man force within the city. But Washington's position seemed hopeless. At best, he had only 5,000 men, and his army's morale was almost at an all-time low. Soldiers were deserting in droves, and few, if any, new volunteers were coming forward.

At last, Washington began sending detachments under Lafayette, Anthony Wayne, and von Steuben down to Virginia to oppose Cornwallis' raiding tactics. Although the American army in Virginia was gradually building up, Cornwallis' superior force continued to win whenever the Americans challenged them.

Cornwallis decided to build a permanent supply base in Virginia from which his army could operate. The little port of Yorktown, on Chesapeake Bay, seemed to be an ideal location. He took his army there in June and began at once to build fortifications.

While all this was going on, a huge French fleet started across the Atlantic, bringing with it several thousand French soldiers. Washington reluctantly gave up his plans to use these reinforcements against Clinton in New York, and decided, instead, to employ them against Cornwallis in Virginia. This decision, made against his better judgment, turned out to be the decisive one of the war. He left a small force in New York in order to fool Clinton into thinking that the bulk of his army was still there, and marched south with his main army. He was joined by 4,500 French regulars under General Rochambeau.

In September of 1781, Washington assembled his armies at Williamsburg, fourteen miles from Yorktown. Almost as though by a miracle of timing and luck, Washington had, instead of the straggly army on which he had been forced to depend since the war's beginning, a combined American-French force of more than 15,000 men. The huge French fleet, having beaten a smaller English one and chased it back to New York, now commanded the entire Bay. Cornwallis, with his army of 7,000, was caught in Yorktown in a trap he had fashioned himself.

Washington at once marched his army to Yorktown and laid siege to the fortifications. From all sides, French and American artillery blasted the British position with an almost twenty-four hour barrage. Cornwallis' supplies of food and ammunition began to run dangerously low. His men were worn out by sickness and the fatigue of the unending bombardment. Only a few thousand were fit enough to man the defense works. At one point Cornwallis made a desperate attempt to escape, but he failed.

There was nothing Cornwallis could do. On October 17, a British officer waving a white flag, and accompanied by a drummer, appeared on top of the fortifications and signaled for a parley. He had a message from the general. Cornwallis wanted to surrender.

Two days later, the British army, marched out of Yorktown to the blaring of their own bands, passed between lines of Frenchmen and Americans, and laid down their arms.

At that very moment, Clinton, with 7,000 men, was on his way to reinforce Cornwallis. But when his fleet arrived off Chesapeake Bay, it was all over. He sailed back to New York.

The conditions of the surrender were in the same terms as those imposed on General Lincoln at the surrender of Charleston. Lincoln was given the honor of overseeing the laying down of arms and the disposal of prisoners.

No one thought that the surrender of Yorktown was the end of the war, least of all, George Washington. Anxious to take advantage of the splendid

General Benjamin Lincoln, who had suffered the shame of the surrender at Charleston, was distinguished by General Washington with the honor of receiving General O'Hara's sword as sign of the surrender of Cornwallis.

forces that had been assembled here for the siege, he tried to persuade the French commanders to join with him in the conquest of New York. But Rochambeau decided to keep his army in Virginia, and the admiral of the French fleet took his ships and troops on to the West Indies. Washington then took his Americans and marched northward to the Hudson.

What discouraged England from continuing the war?

Independence at Last

Yorktown was the last straw. The British had had enough. The king stubbornly wanted to keep on fighting but his ministers demanded that the futile war be ended. It was now apparent that the American colonies could never be subdued.

Besides, the British parliament had plenty of other headaches. England was still at war with France and Spain, and soldiers were desperately needed in the West Indies, Africa and Gibraltar. If the more than 30,000 men stationed in New York, Charleston and Savannah could quickly be sent to the West Indies, for example, it might mean a British victory in those islands.

Furthermore, the war had continued far longer than anyone had imagined possible. The British war debt was mounting. Taxes in England were alarmingly high, and the king's treasury was practically bankrupt. Thus, the English armies were removed from America as rapidly as possible.

Washington disbanded his army and went to live in peace on his Mount Vernon plantation. He intended to remain there for the rest of his life, never dreaming that he would be called back to serve his country again as its first President.

On September 3, 1783, Britain signed the Treaty of Paris, recognizing the United States of America as an independent nation.

With the war over at last, Americans hung up their guns, rolled up their sleeves, and went to work to build a new country — a country that one day would become the spiritual leader of all freedom-loving men the world over.